BRITAIN IN OLD PHOTOGRAPHS

EAST GRINSTEAD

DAVID GOULD

ALAN SUTTON PUBLISHING LIMITED

Alan Sutton Publishing Limited
Phoenix Mill · Far Thrupp · Stroud
Gloucestershire · GL5 2BU

First published 1995

Cover photographs: East Grinstead High Street in about 1928, by which time the motor age was evidently well under way. See also p. 121.

British Library Cataloguing in Publication Data.
A catalogue record for this book is available from the British Library.

ISBN 0-7509-1076-3

Typeset in 9/10 Sabon.
Typesetting and origination by
Alan Sutton Publishing Limited.
Printed in Great Britain by
Hartnolls, Bodmin, Cornwall.

Contents

Harold Connold (1889–1968), East Grinstead's leading professional photographer between 1926 and 1959. This portrait dates from 1949–50, when he was chairman of East Grinstead Urban District Council. (H. Connold)

Introduction

The town of East Grinstead is rather more than 750 years old, photography is a little over 150. These pages might, therefore, be expected to illustrate only the most recent part of the story. In fact, however, they can help us go further back. For instance, many of our oldest surviving houses are still in use after 400 years, with several after 500 years, and a few after more than 600 years. Yet here we can see some of them before their timber frames were uncovered and new doors, windows or shopfronts inserted late in the nineteenth century and at the beginning of the twentieth century, showing us aspects of their earlier structural history about which no written records survive. For many of those buildings that are no longer with us, the camera is our only witness.

The shape of the town and its development can be easily recognized: the High Street with its wide market place, laid out in the early thirteenth century, and then, after the coming of the railway in 1855, development down London Road towards the station and beyond.

More than that, the camera shows us, in ways that written records and buildings cannot, how people used the town, how they lived and what they looked like. The work, leisure activities and celebrations shown here remind us that a town has a life of its own, continuing and adapting through the generations as much as the buildings and the street plan do. We inherit that life and these structures as part of the collective memory that gives our town its identity; just as a person who has lost his memory has lost his identity, so a town that loses its history loses its identity too.

This is why these photographs are so significant, not merely for picturesque or nostalgic qualities, important though these are, nor solely as records for interpretation, but also as contributors to and stimulators of that collective memory and identity. Readers with no previous acquaintance with East Grinstead will catch from this collection as surely as the oldest resident or the latest newcomer much of what has made and still makes the town the place it is. Something of its inhabitants' pride in and care for their heritage may come through too.

One expression of that concern is the work of volunteers in founding and running the Town Museum, from whose collection of over 4,000 photographic images this selection has been made by its Hon. Keeper of Photography. His detailed knowledge of these pictures and assiduity in researching the information needed for their understanding ensure this book's permanent value.

Those whose appetites are whetted will find it ideally complemented by both a visit to the museum at East Court, and by a walk round the routes of the town trails published by the East Grinstead Society. The current town guide gives a potted history and contemporary facts, figures and illustrations. *The History of East Grinstead* by W.H. Hills (see p. 95), published in 1906, is still the standard work.

M.J. Leppard
Hon. Curator of the Town Museum, 1976–93

A Selection of East Grinstead Photographers

William Harding was a professional photographer from around 1862 with an address in the High Street; thanks to him we have an excellent pictorial record of the town's appearance during the 1860s and '70s. He was librarian of the Literary and Scientific Institute (whose building is shown on p. 49) from 1888 until 1922.

Arthur Harding, his son, not only reissued much of William's work as picture postcards in the early to mid-1900s, but also produced a vast amount of his own, including a set of pictures intended for (but not used in) *The History of East Grinstead*. In addition he recorded most of the town's major events photographically and sold the results as postcards in the days before local newspapers carried pictures.

William Page was a professional at Moat Studio, 5 Moat Road, from the 1880s until 1912. His work included studio portraits, miniatures and a large range of local views issued as picture postcards. His predecessor at the same premises in the 1870s was H.T. Melville; very little of Melville's work has survived, although some was reprinted by Page.

The East Grinstead Photo Company was the name used by Edgar Kinsey, who was at 24 Railway Approach from around 1906 until the late 1920s. Like Harding he sold postcards of street scenes and major events in the town, and also created studio portraits.

Victor Morris, postmaster and grocer at 65 Lingfield Road, issued several postcards of local views from around 1910, but he was not a professional photographer. Nor was C.S. Jenks, whose name appears on the backs of some surviving pictures from the early 1900s of groups of people. Jenks was in fact an architect, who lived at 34 Cantelupe Road between 1909 and 1930.

Undoubtedly the most artistic and technically proficient of all East Grinstead's professional photographers was Harold Thomas Connold. Born in Hastings on 26 May 1889, he moved to East Grinstead where he studied photography under Ernest Watts at 23 High Street. In 1926 he took over this business and from then on practically had the field to himself, undertaking portraiture and many other commissions as well as photographing local views, many of which were later issued as postcards. He moved to 15 High Street when Barclays Bank – who owned the new premises – was built in 1934. A member of the Institute of British Photographers and a Rotarian, he served on the Urban District Council, of which he was chairman from 1949 to 1950. After his retirement in June 1959 he left the town, and he died at Herstmonceux on 22 May 1968. According to Malcolm Powell, his former assistant who succeeded to the business, he was not the easiest of people to work for. When giving instructions he would take a long time to come to the point and to say what was actually required – but what superb pictures he has left us!

David Gould

Section One

STREET SCENES

High Street looking east, with Middle Row on the right, early 1900s. The left-hand building was considerably altered to become Young's draper's shop, but Dixon's, further along, was little changed. (Wm Page)

High Street, *c.* 1870. The building seen end on to the street was replaced in 1877. Albion House, on the left, lasted until the early 1930s, being replaced by Barclays Bank in 1934. (H.T. Melville)

High Street at the corner of London Road, showing Fred Maplesden's printing works and the post office. The left-hand part was replaced around 1897 by an extension of Lloyds Bank, Maplesden having moved into the former post office when the new one opened in London Road in 1896.

High Street looking north-east, from behind Constitutional Buildings, early 1900s. The drinking fountain – just visible – was erected in 1887. (Wm Page)

High Street looking east, with a three-wheeled motor car passing two carts, *c.* 1913. Greenstede House, in the centre, was built for George Bailye the tailor in 1877, and about twenty years later was acquired by Alec Johnson, another tailor, who remained there until 1920. (E. Batstone)

High Street and Middle Row, 1921. The former tailor's shop of 1877 has now become a branch of the London Joint City and Midland Bank, and in 1995 it is still the main branch of Midland Bank in the town. (F. Frith & Co.)

High Street looking east from 2 London Road, 1927. The further extension of Lloyds Bank (1921) is on the left, and replaced Maplesden's at 3 High Street. Part of Constitutional Buildings, built in 1893, is on the right. (F. Frith & Co.)

The south side of High Street, with the premises of plumber and ironmonger W.H. Steer, 1870s. The fifteenth-century building on their right was demolished in 1968, despite the fact that it was listed and in reasonable condition. The replacement re-used some of the original material. (Wm Harding)

High Street, south side, with harbingers of the advancing motor age evident, mid-1920s. The lime trees, planted in 1874, were a responsibility of the Urban District Council.

The south side of High Street, behind Middle Row, early 1900s. Part of the Dorset Arms is on the left. The fifteenth-century building in the centre is no. 46, belonging to G.H. Lynn the stonemason. To the right, at nos 42–4, is W. Stockdale's restaurant, in a sixteenth-century structure.

The Side Walk in the High Street, *c*. 1946. This was the title given by the postcard publisher to this west-facing view. It is dominated by one of the lime trees of 1874. (F. Frith & Co.)

The east end of High Street, with the buildings on the south side, late nineteenth century. Prominent on the centre right is the house of Edward Lynn, builder and undertaker, its timber framing yet to be exposed. (Wm Page)

High Street from the east end, looking west, *c.* 1870. The tall Cromwell House of 1599 with its three chimneys is prominent and on the extreme right is The Rose beerhouse. (H.T. Melville)

The south side of High Street, 1933. On the left is Sackville House (whose timber framing was exposed during restoration in 1919), followed by Amherst House, Dorset House and the Dorset Arms. (F. Frith & Co.)

The top of London Road, towards the end of the nineteenth century. Two carts are outside the Swan Inn, which was in existence by 1709 and by 1882 was owned by Dashwood & Co.

Arthur Harding's little joke: 'Dudley's Newspaper Train'. No wonder the street musician and bystanders in London Road seem unconcerned – the train was never really there, even in 1910, this being a clever piece of photo-montage. (A. Harding)

London Road from the top end, looking north. The two Edwardian ladies walking purposefully up the middle of the road appear to be demonstrating that their town was built for people, not vehicles. (A.H. Homewood, Burgess Hill)

Heavy motor traffic has taken over London Road – and this is 1929! The Swan Hotel, now owned by Tamplin's, had its frontage altered before 1907, but was closed in February 1963 and replaced by shops. (H. Connold)

London Road from the top, with the Swan on the left, Lloyds Bank on the right and the then-new Whitehall in the distance, *c.* 1938. (J. Valentine)

Businesses in London Road celebrate Queen Victoria's Diamond Jubilee, June 1897.

A vanished scene: cottages on the west side of London Road (approximately where no. 32 now stands) and a builder's yard, 1911. (A. Harding)

London Road, *c.* 1920. On the right are Mrs Walker's shoeshop at no. 60 and F. Blanchard's drapery at no. 62. On the left are Grosvenor Hall and the Whitehall Picture Palace. (J. Valentine)

London Road looking south-east, and the Railway Hotel, which opened in 1856. The Glen Vue Road street sign dates the picture to no later than 1906, the year the road was renamed Railway Approach. (A.H. Homewood, Burgess Hill)

London Road and the Railway Hotel, looking towards Glen Vue Road, *c.* 1905. The elm trees were removed in 1925, and the hotel in 1938, being replaced by the Glanfield in 1939. The hotel is now the Broadway. (H. Daniels)

London Road, looking south-east near the junction of Station Road, early 1900s. On the left is the Southdown & East Grinstead Brewery. (H.H. Camburn, Tunbridge Wells)

Blackwell Hollow, *c.* 1906. To this day it is still dominated by trees, but because of heavy motor traffic it is not as good a place for a rest as it was in Edwardian times. (H. Daniels)

Church Lane, often shown in old directories as Church Street. These charming old cottages still survive as offices. No. 8, at the far end, has been the offices of Pearless, de Rougemont, solicitors, since the 1880s. This scene appears to date from the 1900s.

De la Warr Road had not been built when this picture was taken in 1883. The open space in the foreground, Chequer Mead, is now occupied by the Parish Halls. On the right are the National Schools with the headmaster's house. The block on the left later became the Wallis Centre. (Wm Harding)

Durkins Road, off Lingfield Road, *c.* 1905. The houses here, as in Dormans Park Road and St John's Road, were built by George Webb, who died in March 1924. (Wm Page)

Hermitage Lane, looking north. From 1894 the lane was named after The Hermitage, an eighteenth-century house that was pulled down in the late 1970s. In the sixteenth century the road was called Hollow Lane and in the eighteenth and nineteenth centuries was known as Brewhouse Lane. This is an early twentieth-century view.

Imberhorne Lane, looking south-west, *c.* 1920. No. 29, with the enlarged window, was once a tiny shop. The houses were demolished in the 1960s.

King Street, 1937. Laid out in 1934–5, the street's focal point was the Radio Centre cinema, which opened on 11 April 1936. The other buildings include Boots the Chemist, Caffyn's motor garage, which opened in November 1936, and the Jubilee Institute, after which Institute Walk was named. (F. Frith & Co.)

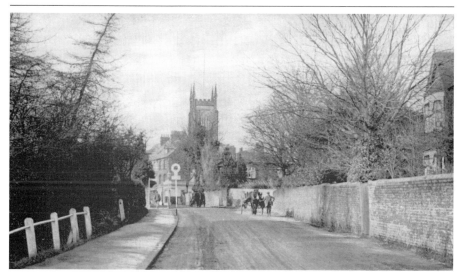

Lewes Road looking west, *c.* 1914. St Swithun's church tower and its tall flagpole are prominent. On the left is the well-remembered post-and-rail fencing, which was only recently removed. (Photochrom, Tunbridge Wells)

New Road after a snowfall in the 1880s. The road was built in about 1826 to give a better-graded access to the eastern end of the town than Old Road. It was later renamed Lewes Road. The fencing crossing from left to right shows the line of the Three Bridges to Tunbridge Wells railway which tunnelled beneath the road.

The northern end of Lingfield Road, early 1900s. At this time the Prince of Wales, which opened in 1863, was just across the county boundary in Surrey. (A. Harding)

Portland Road, looking south. By the 1890s several large villas for the wealthier tradesmen of the town had been built in this road, which originally opened only on to Ship Street. (Wm Page)

Queen's Road, looking north-east, early 1900s. Until 1887 this was called Cemetery Road. All the houses still exist in 1995 except for the group partly obscured by the lamppost. These cottages were pulled down in 1969 in order to create space for a huge car park.

Station Road, looking south towards the station, *c.* 1905. In the distance are the High Level platforms, which closed in 1967 and were dismantled in 1968. (A. Harding)

West Street, looking north-east, *c.* 1913. The flagpole on the church tower helps to date the picture. The house on the right, no. 78, still survives in 1995, despite a demolition threat in 1973. (East Grinstead Photo Co.)

The bottom of Old Mill Hill, 1876, looking south-west to Coombe Hill where Brooklands Way now comes in. Old Mill Hill was later renamed West Hill, and Coneybury, the house on the right, is now named White Cross. (Wm Harding)

Section Two

COMMERCE

Joseph Rice sitting in the doorway of his shop, which was illuminated by gas, early 1900s.

The photographer has recorded that this exposure was made at 10.30 p.m. Rice Bros, cycle

factors and makers of agricultural implements, were at 27–31 London Road until 1943.

The firm also had branches in many parts of south-east England. (A. Harding)

The Crown Hotel, High Street, 1880s. The boarded-up building on the left is presumably about to be demolished to make way for the exit of Cantelupe Road. (Wm Harding)

The seventeenth-century Dorset Arms, *c.* 1870. Originally called the Newe Inn, it was later the Ounce, and then the Catt. The old houses to the right of the inn were demolished in about 1890 to make way for Portland Road.

The Rose & Crown, *c.* 1937. Shortly after this photograph was taken this eighteenth-century house and the adjoining cottage were knocked down and replaced by a new Rose & Crown. Leonard Gasson, by then the oldest licensee in the town, continued in the new pub for another decade. (H. Connold)

The Swan Inn, at the top end of London Road on the west side, 1892. Brinkhurst the saddlers is on the right. (A. Harding)

The White Lion, London Road, 1860s. At this time the inn was around 300 years old. Later it was considerably rebuilt, being demolished in 1965 and replaced by a new White Lion set back from the road. (Wm Harding)

The Felbridge Hotel, mid-1920s. Lying just inside the Sussex boundary, the hotel was built in 1920–22 to the design of Major Thomas Stewart Inglis FRIBA, DSO, and initially owned by him. Recent extensions have altered its original character. (Donald F. Merrett)

Two views of East Grinstead's Fair in the High Street, around the beginning of the twentieth century. At this time two fairs were held each year, on 21 April and 11 December. Above: ponies at the west end in front of the *c*. 1897 extension of Lloyds Bank, next to Maplesden's printing works. Below: cattle standing where nowadays cars are parked.

The cattle market in Cantelupe Road, behind the Crown, 1905. The date is on the poster on the brick wall. The market, founded by William Rudge in the 1870s, was held every second Thursday, but ceased in December 1970. (A. Harding)

Edward Coughtrey (centre) the hairdresser at 74 London Road, *c.* 1925. He was in business from 1914 until the mid-1960s.

W.H. Dixon, analytical chemist, at 51–3 High Street, 'established 1799'. In October 1878 Walter Henry Dixon joined the business founded by Thomas Palmer, and at this time the shop still bears the title 'Palmer & Dixon'. It closed on 11 May 1974.

C. & H. Gasson Ltd were builders' merchants who were in business at 153 London Road from 1894 until 1 January 1980. This picture was taken probably just before the premises were rebuilt in 1895. (Wm Harding)

George Knight's old smithy on the west side of London Road, shortly before closure in 1911. Three shops (the present nos 48, 50 and 52) were later built on this site. Knight lived in Grove House, West Street. (A. Harding)

L.G. Payne's shop at 92 Glen Vue Road sold boots and shoes in the early 1900s, as shown here, but closed before 1910. It is currently a music shop. The road's name was changed to Railway Approach in 1906. (A. Harding)

Robert Pink's cabinet and upholstery warehouse, with shop, on London Road, 1866. Built partly on the site of the old workhouse, which was demolished in 1864, it was replaced in 1883 by the Grosvenor Hall and in 1936 by the Whitehall. (Wm Harding)

A stack of shell cases at the Rice Bros works, which the government had asked the firm to make in 1915. On the left stands Thomas Robert Playfoot who, being a skilled engineer, was not called up during the First World War.

Southdown & East Grinstead Brewery on London Road, March 1906. Previously the Hope Brewery, it was acquired by Southdown & East Grinstead Breweries Ltd in 1895, and was rebuilt three years later. It closed in 1920, and was adapted by the UDC for its new offices, fire station and electricity generating station, and was approximately where the fire station now stands.

Inside one of the sheds of John Stenning & Son's timber yard, where tennis racquets are being made, 1930s. The yard, which was located where Sussex House now stands, closed in 1965.

Streatfield's fruit and vegetable shop at 190 London Road operated between 1914 and 1938. There were also Streatfield shops at 20 Railway Approach from 1909 to 1913, and at 32 London Road from 1912 to 1928. Note the boldly lettered prices that used to be such a characteristic of fruiterers' shops.

W. Stone was a poulterer at 44, 46 and 48 Railway Approach until around 1914. This small-scale business was apparently conducted from the front room of his house. The sight of plucked chickens hanging in the open would no doubt be objected to nowadays.

John Tully owned this chemist's and stationer's shop in London Road on the corner of Glen Vue Road from 1870. By 1906, when the road was renamed Railway Approach, the shop had been taken over by W.H. Dixon & Sons, who ran it until the 1970s. (Wm Harding)

Percy Edward Tombs, stationer and publisher of local view cards, was at 18 London Road from around 1908 until 1910, when he briefly managed the Railway Hotel. Next door is Charles Morton Wilson's furniture and carpet warehouse, which in 1913 was converted into the Cinema de Luxe.

Francis Moore Wilcox, saddler and harness maker (established in 1881), was at 73 High Street, on the corner of Church Lane, for many years. He died in April 1936, but the business was carried on by his son Harold until the mid-1950s.

Section Three

BUILDINGS

The south-east aspect of Sackville College, 1860s. The college was founded in 1608 by

Robert, Earl of Dorset, as an institution for the poor, and was in use by 1619, having 31

residents, 21 men and 10 women. (J.C. Stenning, 1839–1922)

Two residents enjoying the sunshine outside the south door of Sackville College, August 1855. One of the Revd J.M. Neale's daughters is sitting on the left. This picture is thought to be the work of Joseph Cundall (1818–95).

The north front of Sackville College, early 1900s. The belfry is a nineteenth-century 'restoration', made after the original was blown down in a storm on 26 November 1703. (Wm Page)

The reconstructed Sackville College chapel. Its foundation stone was laid on 1 August 1850. Here sermons were preached by J.M. Neale, the warden of Sackville College from 1846 to 1866.

Sackville College common room, probably in the early 1930s. The text on the wall above the fireplace is still there today. (H. Connold)

Sackville College hall which, with its splendid furniture and carved woodwork, would not disgrace a stately home.

Dorset House in the High Street, 1930s. So-named since the 1880s, this fine brick-fronted town house dates from 1705, although the dormer windows are nineteenth-century additions. In recent years the house has been converted into offices.

Judges Terrace, 1860s. On the right is the seventeenth-century Old Stone House, before its westward extension. Next door is Clarendon House which dates from around 1500. In 1939 the timber framing of Clarendon House was exposed to view. (Wm Harding)

No. 53 High Street, a sixteenth-century weatherboarded building of a type often found in Kent. On the left is part of W.H. Dixon & Sons' shop front. The lady in the doorway is possibly Mrs Dixon, who is recorded as having lived next door with Percy Dixon at Gothic House, no. 55, between 1915 and 1928.

The Jubilee Institute, London Road, which opened in November 1888. Built of local sandstone to the design of Paul B. Chambers, it was the headquarters of the Literary and Scientific Institute, a library-cum-debating society, and lasted until 1937. On the right are the cottages known as Rock Gardens, demolished between 1934 and 1935. (A. Harding)

A painting (artist unknown) of Placeland, an eighteenth-century house in large grounds on the north-east side of London Road, looking south-east. The solicitor Arthur Hastie lived here. He was assistant warden of Sackville College from 1878 until his death in November 1901. (A. Harding)

This house on London Road, at the corner of Green Hedges Avenue, was used as the Local Board and the Urban District Council offices until 1922. The site is now East Grinstead Tyre Service. (A. Harding)

Halsford, the residence of William Vicesimus Knox Stenning. Stenning was the first chairman of the Constitutional Club (from 1890) and also chairman of the Gas & Water Co. in the 1900s. John Cuthbert Stenning, author of *Notes on East-Grinstead* in 1868, was born here in 1839.

The Dovecote and Gatehouse, built in about 1862 and photographed when only a couple of years old. The private drive which the Gatehouse guarded led to Hurst-an-Clays, the home of Charles Chevall Tooke until his death in October 1890. (Wm Harding)

The Dovecote and Gatehouse, c. 1928. The early starkness has worn off, plants have grown and subsequent alterations to the house have not reduced its picturesque charm. (J. Valentine)

The south elevation of East Court. The house was built in 1769 for John Cranston and passed to Edward Cranston in 1781. It was sold to Ernest Cooper around 1906, and passed through several ownerships from 1927. In 1946 it became the UDC offices and from April 1974 those of the Town Council. (Wm Page)

The south elevation of Imberhorne. The house was built in the late 1870s, and here has a later extension to the left. Sir Edward Blount (1809–1905), chairman of the Western Railway of France, lived here. After his grandson Mr E.C. Blount died the house was demolished in about 1956, and the grounds sold for building the present Imberhorne estate. (A. Harding)

Green Hedges, *c.* 1933. In the 1860s and '70s this was the home of John Henry Rogers, the founder and first doctor of the nearby cottage hospital in 1863. He was also warden of Sackville College from 1872 until his death in October 1879. (H. Connold)

Moat House, *c.* 1888. This house was built in 1877 on the north-west side of Moat Road, approximately where nos 18–20 now stand, and lasted until the 1950s. For several years it was the home of E.P. Whitley Hughes, a solicitor and part-time clerk to the UDC.

Wellington Town cottages, looking north-east from the path that still runs from the former Charlwoods Row (now Charlwoods Road) to Green Hedges Avenue, *c.* 1905. Believed to date from the seventeenth century, the cottages were demolished in September 1963 and light industry now occupies their site. (Wm Page)

Zion Cottage, at 1 Ship Street. Later called Corner Cottage, it was demolished in the middle of 1934. On the left is the Ship Inn, known as the Spread Eagle until the late seventeenth century. (Wm Page)

Coneybury Lodge on Coombe Hill or Turners Hill Road, looking north, 1890s. The house in the background on the right, Coneybury, is now called White Cross. The lodge is now Old Mill Cottages, which were extended at the left-hand end in 1980. (Smith & Co.)

The post-mill on East Grinstead Common, shortly before its demise, *c.* 1900. Windmill Lane and a house named Millfield perpetuate its memory.

Section Four

CHURCHES, SCHOOLS
AND HOSPITALS

*The east elevation of St Swithun's parish church, 1900s. St Swithun was Bishop of
Winchester from 852 to 862. This church, on the site of an earlier one, was built largely
in the 1790s to the design of James Wyatt in 'battlemented Perpendicular style'.*

(Davidson Bros)

St Swithun's tower, designed by J.T. Groves, as seen from Portland Road. The old gentleman is said to be the Revd Douglas Yeoman Blakiston, who was vicar from 1871 to 1908. (Wm Page)

St Swithun's church from the south-east, *c.* 1913. The stone used in its construction was taken from Blackwell, Selsfield and Wych Cross. The churchyard was closed for further burials in 1866. (E. Batstone)

The interior of St Swithun's. At the eastern end of the north aisle is the organ which was taken from St Margaret's Convent in 1888, and lasted until 1936. The chancel screen, which was erected in 1915, is not yet in place. (Wm Page)

St Mary's Anglican Church, Windmill Lane. The foundation stone was laid on 7 July 1891, but construction of the brick-built church was protracted and it was not completed until 1912. The photograph was taken shortly afterwards. (V.E. Morris)

St Mary's Church clergymen and servers. Can they be identified?

The interior of the Church of St Mary the Virgin, looking west, 1913. Consecration took place in 1905. The screen has since been moved.

The Roman Catholic Church of Our Lady and St Peter, 1925. The church was opened on 2 October 1898, its cost being met by Lady Blount of Imberhorne. (F. Frith & Co.)

The interior of the Church of Our Lady and St Peter. The initials in the stonework over the main door, MR and SP, stand for *Maria Regina* and *Sanctus Petrus*. (H. Connold)

Moat Congregational Church, *c*. 1910. It was built by Edward Steer, himself a Congregationalist, on land sold by him in 1868; the church was opened on 5 April 1870, and the hall was added in 1905–6. It is now the United Reformed Church. (East Grinstead Photo Co.)

The Revd W. Hipkin, minister of Moat Church from April 1900 to July 1903, is second from the left at the back of this large group of people, who are possibly on an outing. (C.S. Jenks)

Moat Congregational Church Bible class, 1911. Unfortunately, so far no one has been identified.

In January 1930 one of the four pinnacles on the parish church tower was blown down, falling through the roof. The repairs were carried out by Brooker Bros, local builders, and all the pinnacles were shortened and strengthened. The verger, Mr Jones, is on the right. (H. Connold)

Zion Chapel, West Street, *c.* 1880. Its foundation stone was laid on 2 July 1810, and the opening took place on 23 April 1811. The chapel's appearance has been altered by the addition of a low, flat-roofed frontage, and the manse on the left has vanished.

The interior of Zion Chapel. Until 1847 this was the only Nonconformist place of worship in the town, having been paid for by the Countess of Huntingdon's Trust. Since February 1981 it has been Zion Baptist Church.

The north-west front of St Margaret's Anglican Convent, which was ready for occupation in 1870. The chapel, opened in 1883, has a saddleback tower of a type found in South Wales, and its architect, G.E. Street, built churches there also. (H. Connold)

Orphans from St Margaret's Convent holding crosses on the steps of the south side of High Street, 1911. (East Grinstead Photo Co.)

John Mason Neale (1818–66). In July 1855 Neale founded the Anglican Society of St Margaret, whose sisters ministered to the sick poor. A prolific writer and hymnologist, he was ordained in 1842, later becoming a Doctor of Divinity.

Dr Neale's daughter, Ermenild, who was Mother Superior at St Margaret's Convent from August 1902 until her resignation in 1932. She was well loved by all, especially the children to whom she was known as Mother Bunny.

The National Schools, not long after their opening on 1 January 1861. At first under the control of the Revd C.W.P. Crawfurd, from 1875 they came under a School Board. When the County Council took over the running of the Board Schools they were renamed the Council Schools.

The girls' class in the Council Schools, early 1900s. The schools were extended and in recent times renamed Chequer Mead. However, closure came about in July 1990.

A class from Imberhorne (Roman Catholic) school, c. 1907. This was established by Sir Edward Blount in 1895. He wrote in 1902 that about eighty children attended, including Protestants, 'because they appreciate the teaching'.

An Imberhorne school play, 1900s. None of the cast has been identified, not even those inside the realistic-looking bear costumes. (A. Harding)

A group from the Modern School, 1924. The school, at 14–16 Cantelupe Road, was founded in 1894 by the Revd Robert Bidwell Matson for the sons of tradesmen and professional people. Matson was headmaster until 1910, and died in March 1936. The successor headmaster, Frederic Newcombe, is sitting in the middle, straw-hatted and looking every bit as fierce as Mr Matson had done. To his left is Edward F. Tuite, who by 1928 was the headmaster in his turn.

East Grinstead's first cottage hospital, which opened in October 1863, accommodating seven patients. However, it closed in 1874. The actual cottage, at the end of Green Hedges Avenue, still survives and is believed to date from the eighteenth century. (A. Harding)

Lansdowne House, London Road. Built in 1887 at the corner of Garland Road, it was the town's second cottage hospital when it opened on 11 January 1888. When it was no longer required it was sold in about 1902 to W.H. Hills, the journalist, who lived there until the mid-1920s. (A. Harding)

The third cottage hospital, Queen's Road, 1911. It was opened on 15 October 1902, having been converted from 'Holiday Home No. 2' of the Ragged School Union. It had been built in 1879 as the Elephant's Head coffee tavern – an unsuccessful venture. The matron from 1910 until 1936 was Miss Leonora Garlett. (F. Frith & Co.)

The Queen Victoria Cottage Hospital, when new in 1936. It was opened by Princess Helena Victoria on 8 January 1936, in heavy rain. This is the Holtye Road (south-east) frontage, which is over 300 ft long. (H. Connold)

The south-west elevation of Queen Victoria Cottage Hospital, 1936. This superseded the old Queen's Road establishment. The land for building was donated by Sir Robert Kindersley. (H. Connold)

The Kindersley men's ward at the time of opening, 1936. The 'cottage' part of the title was soon dropped, and many more wings have been added to the original structure since the Second World War. (H. Connold)

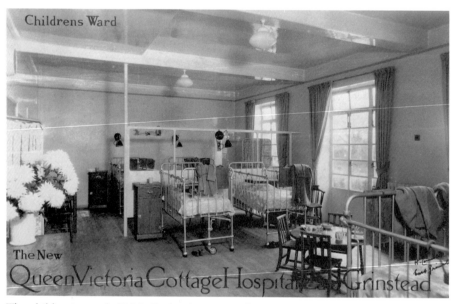

The children's ward, 1936. For a short time the matron was Miss Garlett, who had transferred from Queen's Road, but she soon retired and she died on 7 September 1939. (H. Connold)

NOTABLE EVENTS

The Coronation of King George V was marked in East Grinstead by this superb procession,

seen here in London Road from the vantage point of Rock Gardens, 22 June 1911.

Among the celebrations in June 1897 of Queen Victoria's 60 years' reign was this vast bonfire on Mason's Field. This open space became Grosvenor and Crescent Roads in 1905. (Wm Page)

Celebrating the Coronation of Edward VII at Mrs George Read's furniture store, 19–21 London Road, 9 August 1902. The firm was in business here from 1886 to 1944.

Joseph Rice, with his family and supporters in London Road, celebrating after he came top of the poll with 407 votes in the UDC election of 1901. On the left is part of the offices of the *East Grinstead Observer*. (A. Harding)

Declaration of General Election results from Rock Gardens, London Road, 26 January 1906. Uniquely, the Liberal candidate, C.H. Corbett, won the seat, but four years later H.S. Cautley (Conservative) took it, and was to hold it until 1936. (A. Harding)

The ruins of the vicarage after a disastrous fire, 27 February 1908. The brigade had been called promptly, but owing to feeble water pressure its efforts were in vain and the men had to watch helplessly as the fire took hold. (Wm Page)

Firemen sadly surveying the wreckage of the vicarage, which was only about 50 years old. The vicar, D.Y. Blakiston, lost many valuable articles in the fire and was heartbroken. He resigned the living later that year. (A. Harding)

The first meet of the Burstow hounds outside the Dorset Arms Hotel, November 1911. Whatever one's feelings about hunting, there is no denying that it makes a scene of pictorial interest. (East Grinstead Photo Co.)

The Working Men's Club annual rabbit-pie supper in Queen's Hall, *c.* 1920. The hall opened in 1899, and it was at one of these suppers that Joseph Rice choked on a rabbit bone – fortunately a doctor was at hand. The club was founded in about 1893 by R.B. Matson, founder of the Modern School. (East Grinstead Photo Co.)

Soldiers riding along Lingfield Road, past the recreation ground, at around the time of the outbreak of the First World War in August 1914, presumably bound for France. The boy in the road casting an admiring glance at the splendid sight is Tom Buckland (1907–83), who was later to work at the East Grinstead Gas & Water Co. (V.E. Morris)

The funeral of the Revd W.W. Handford, vicar of St Mary's Church from 1893 to 1918. The cortège is passing Placeland in London Road, A.H. Hastie's residence.

A procession in London Road to celebrate Peace Day, 19 July 1919. The Volunteer & Town Band is followed by the fire brigade, behind which is the huge banner of 'Court Hand in Hand' of the Ancient Order of Foresters.

A captured German gun in Dunnings Mill Pond. The gun was the property of the UDC and had been tipped into the pond on 24 April 1920 by some men who felt that its display in the High Street was an affront to ex-servicemen. The schoolboy is Roy Sherlock, who was to become an irrigation engineer in the Sudan. (Ken Nutt)

Collecting for the Cottage Hospital outside the post office in London Road, 29 July 1922. These fund-raising annual occasions were known as 'Hospital Saturdays'. (East Grinstead Photo Co.)

Cromwell House on fire, 9 December 1928. Only the shell of the house remained, but it was rebuilt in 1929 with several modifications. (H. Connold)

Imberhorne Farm Cottages, on the north-west side of Imberhorne Lane, after being struck by lightning on 24 June 1926. The centre chimney was wrecked and a resident, Mrs Pollard, suffered injury.

Laying the foundation stone of the Parish Hall, 9 June 1929. The ceremony was performed by Isabella Moir. Also present was the Revd Dr Golding Golding-Bird, vicar from September 1925 until 1954. (H. Connold)

An open-air service in the High Street in memory of the three East Grinstead martyrs who were burned in June 1556. The service was organised by the Sussex Martyrs' Commemoration Council and is believed to have been held in June 1929. (H. Connold)

Messrs W.J. Armstrong's entry for the procession that celebrated the Jubilee of King George V, 6 May 1935. Their wine merchant's business has been run from the same shop in London Road for over a hundred years.

Destruction by enemy action of Bridglands and Rice Bros buildings in London Road, 9 July 1943. The Whitehall cinema was destroyed with heavy loss of life, although the frontage survived, as can be seen in the left background. On the right is the Warwick Arms. At the top of the turntable ladder is fireman Fred Puddephat. (*East Grinstead Observer*)

London Road was hit again on 12 July 1944. This time a 'pilotless aircraft' or flying bomb was shot down, completing the destruction of the shops to the south-east of the Whitehall, as well as the Warwick Arms. King George VI and Queen Elizabeth are being shown around by the head ARP warden, T.P. Peters (standing behind the queen).

Not Dresden, but what remained of London Road after the damage of both July 1943 and July 1944, viewed towards the south-west.

A VE day street party in Queen's Road, 8 May 1945. The party was attended by about fifty local children.

Section Six

PEOPLE

Dr Spencer Lewis Walker, Scoutmaster of the 1st East Grinstead Scouts from their formation in 1908 until the late 1930s. By 1936 the Scouts were famed throughout Sussex for their hand-carved oak heraldic shields. Dr Walker, who from the late 1920s lived at Old Stone House, Judges Terrace, also served on the Urban District Council and was its chairman in 1937/8 (probably the date of this portrait) and from 1942 to 1944.

(H. Connold)

The East Grinstead Fire Brigade, which was first formed in 1863, posing in front of the north door of Sackville College. The new horse-drawn engine dated from 1884, probably when this picture was taken, and was still in use in 1906. (Wm Page)

The town's fire station was at 140 London Road between 1906 and 1922. Left to right: George Simmons, Tom Simmons, Captain William Simmons, E. Perrin.

The East Grinstead Fire Brigade won the South Coast Challenge Shield in 1913. The men, with their Shand Mason engine, are at the rear of the fire station at 140 London Road. (A. Harding)

Post office staff of the early twentieth century, the ladies displaying some glorious headwear. The bowler-hatted postmaster is W. Cleaver, Henry Evershed sports a straw hat, and the three telegraph boys sitting at the front are E. Draper, F. Winter and D. Thomas.

Men at work in Moat Road taking a breather in order to be photographed, possibly in the 1920s. In the background are the houses in St John's Road, which date from 1900.

John Stenning & Son's employees at the timber yard, about to set off for a works outing to the British Empire Exhibition at Wembley, 25 July 1924.

Revd Charles Walter Payne Crawfurd, c. 1896. Mr Crawfurd was chairman of the Local Board from August 1884 to December 1894, and was first chairman of the Urban District Council from then until August 1895. Born at Saint Hill on 14 March 1826, he was ordained in 1850 and lived at East Court for several years. This great public figure died on 10 March 1909.

A sample of Payne Crawfurd's handwriting, 1903. This is written on the back of the photograph above. As the lay rector he owned the chancel of St Swithun's Church. When in September 1874 the vicar requested leave to have two holes made in the chancel floor for gas pipes, Payne Crawfurd immediately replied: 'I can allow no alterations whatsoever in the chancel nor can I give leave for the perforation for gas pipes.'

Arthur Edwin Evershed, East Grinstead's oldest pensioner postman, on holiday in Great Yarmouth, *c.* 1938. He lived at 153 West Street from the early 1900s to the 1960s. (Cine Snaps, Great Yarmouth)

Wallace Henry Hills (1863 – 1932), *c.* 1905. Hills was editor of the *East Grinstead Observer* and a noted local historian, being author of *The History of East Grinstead*, which was published in 1906. As a journalist he permeated the town: he was on the UDC (four times as chairman), was a director of several local companies, and was a churchwarden of St Mary's.

Richard Pennifold, a pastrycook and confectioner until the mid-1920s. He was a committed Nonconformist who was deacon of Moat Church. In 1886 his premises were at 4 Moat Terrace (now 193 London Road), but by 1910 he had moved to 1 St James's Road. He died on 25 December 1929.

Fred Pennifold, Richard's son, who lived as a recluse on the second floor of 1 St James's Road (later 174 London Road). Apart from playing the mandolin he practised astrology. This picture is thought to date from just after the First World War.

Admiral Sir Charles Madden GCB, *c.* 1927. During the First World War he was commander of the Atlantic fleet, and in 1919 became a baronet. He lived at Herontye in Lewes Road from June 1921 to January 1926, and was a St Swithun's churchwarden from 1925 to 1927. He unveiled the new war memorial in the High Street on 23 July 1922, and died in June 1935. (Hay Wrightson Ltd)

Dr Spencer Lewis Walker in his First World War uniform. Until around 1916 this wealthy bachelor and Scoutmaster lived at the now-vanished Woodstock House in London Road, on the north corner of Garland Road.

Mrs Wigney of Southwick House, London Road, on Mist in the stableyard of Nutt Bros in the early 1920s. When riding she would lash out with her whip at anyone who got in her way! (K. Nutt)

Nutt's coachmen appear to be raring to go as they are surveyed by their employer, Harold Hewitt Nutt, in the stableyard at Station Road. The second coachman from the left is Charles Baker.

East Grinstead Home Guard No. IV Platoon, 'A' Company, in front of the pavilion on West Street cricket ground, *c.* 1941. The ground was sold for building in 1988. (H. Connold)

A Civil Defence field kitchen, set up on the Playfield for bombed-out people or evacuees passing through, *c.* 1943. On the left is Mrs P. Carter, and in the background is the Council School. The Playfield became a 'temporary' car park in 1992. (*Kent & Sussex Courier*)

Section Seven

RECREATION AND
SPORT

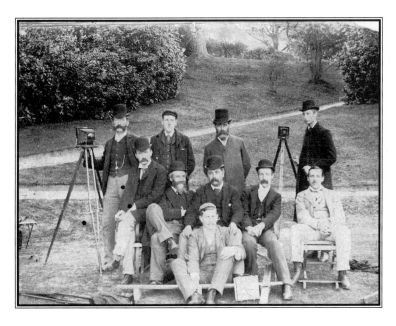

The East Grinstead Photographic Society, some time between 1888 and 1895.

The East Grinstead Operatic Society's presentation of *The Pirates of Penzance* at the Whitehall Theatre, January 1932. The society was formed in 1922 and its musical director until 1939 was Dora Powell, who lived at Oakcroft, Moat Road. She is featured in Elgar's *Enigma Variations* as 'Dorabella'.

The Grosvenor Hall, London Road, decorated for the Coronation of Edward VII, 9 August 1902. The hall was first used on 11 February 1884, and later became the Whitehall Theatre, Picture Palace and the Grosvenor Restaurant. (A. Harding)

A much enlarged Whitehall, replacing both the old Grosvenor Hall and Rock Gardens to its left, was opened on 16 November 1936. It incorporated a cinema, restaurant, ballroom and three shops.

The Cinema de Luxe was converted in 1913 from a building that had started life in 1875 as the Public Hall. *Sally of the Sawdust*, starring W.C. Fields, was shown in September 1925 and was imaginatively promoted by the cinema staff.

St Swithun's bellringers outside the west door of the church, 6 May 1935. Back row, left to right: Thomas Tullett, George Tizzard, Ernest Ladd, Herbert Whyte, George Lambert, Sidney Chesson. Front row: Joseph Wren, Dr G. Golding-Bird (vicar), Miss K.M. Shepherd.

The East Grinstead handbell ringers, *c.* 1900.

The East Grinstead Volunteer and Town Band with its president, Dr Charles Henry Gatty, at his home, Felbridge Place, 1890s. The Town Band and the Volunteer Band had amalgamated in about 1890.

The Cricket Club, 1892. Back row, left to right: J. Charlwood, S. Lucena, R.P. Crawfurd (secretary), E. Whitley Hughes, W.J. Stenning, Alan Huggett. Middle row: E. Charlwood, A. Payne, C. Charlwood, Fred Maplesden. Front row: Arthur Huggett, H. Tebay, W. Payne.

The Hockey Club, c. 1912. Standing, second from right, is the Revd W.E. Sealy, who was assistant master and later head of Fonthill School. On the far left is Alec Johnson, the tailor, of 1–2 Middle Row.

The Football Club, 1923–4 season. Back row, second from left, is Bob Burgess, a machinist at the *East Grinstead Observer's* printing works. To the right of Stan Leppard (holding the ball) is Fred Gear, who was a skilled signwriter and an employee of Brooker Bros, builders and decorators, for fifty years.

The Scouts' gymnastic display on Mount Noddy during the Coronation celebrations, May 1937. (Mrs A.M. Leppard)

Brooklands Park open-air swimming pool. Opened on 8 June 1935, it was an enlargement of the original pool built in 1911. It closed in the late 1970s.

The British Legion billiards team posing in the Sackville College quadrangle, *c*. 1935. The team won the challenge shield and cups in the Edenbridge and District Games League. (H. Connold)

The Whist Club with a candelabrum trophy, 1914.

A glider designed and constructed by the 1st East Grinstead Scouts about to be launched near Hurst-an-Clays, spring 1912. Most of the work was done by George Smith and Tom Beard. Clays Close, off Ship Street, now covers the field.

Section Eight

TRANSPORT

W.H. Dixon & Sons' Thornycroft delivery lorry in the High Street, 1912. Crates of
Dixon's own mineral water are being loaded outside their High Street works. The firm
claimed to be the first in East Grinstead to adopt motor delivery, which began in 1912.
(East Grinstead Photo Co.)

The delivery cart of W. Curtis, the baker, early 1900s. The bakery was at 16 De la Warr Road, and there were shops in London Road and West Street.

Nutt's conveyance, with two horses and driver Charles Baker. The group is within the grounds of the Southdown & East Grinstead Breweries Ltd, London Road. (G. Winchester)

Hall & Co.'s coal delivery cart, attended by 'Lively' Cooper, paying a visit to the stableyard of Nutt Bros in Station Road, early 1920s. (K. Nutt)

Nutt Bros' brougham, with Timothy Waymark, in the stableyard off Station Road, *c*. 1922. (K. Nutt)

Nutt's French victoria awaiting custom in the station forecourt. The three drivers – Charles Baker, George Terry and George Leppard – are enjoying the 1921 sunshine. Nutt Bros had exclusive cab rights at the station from 1905. (K. Nutt)

William Best & Son's Foster steam tractor, *c.* 1910. On the left in the coal merchants' Park Road yard is the founder, and standing by the wheel is one of his sons, Albert, who was to continue the business until 1975.

Mrs George Read's first motor delivery van outside Read's warehouse in Queen's Road, presumably when new. The van was built in 1912 by Thornycroft and remained in use until 1923.

Read's second motor delivery van when new, displaying the results of the signwriter's art. Also built by Thornycroft, this van was in use from 1923 to 1929.

Joseph Rice's car outside its owner's home, Wesley House, in Cantelupe Road, *c.* 1910. Mr and Mrs Rice are sitting in the back and Joseph Rice Jnr is at the wheel. Wesley House was demolished in 1985. (A. Harding)

Walter Crapps (1876–1968) and his Godfrey & Nash motor car in Nutt Bros' yard, 7 July 1921. Mr Crapps, who lived in Grosvenor Road, was the organist at St Swithun's and the pianist at the Whitehall cinema. (K. Nutt)

A line-up of hire cars, all Unics, and their drivers in Nutt Bros' yard, *c.* 1923. Left to right: Harry Pavett, Bert Buddle, Walter Payne, Jim Leppard. (K. Nutt)

Nutt's Garage in Station Road, *c.* 1928. The man is Kenneth Nutt, who had by then joined the business. Shell, Mobiloil, British Benzol and Cleveland pumps are evident, the first hand-pump having been installed in 1924.

John Stenning & Son's employees' works outing by charabanc, 1920s.

Frank Cooper's 'Pioneer' bus outside Grassmere in Forest View Road, 1920s. His was the first motor-bus service between East Grinstead and Tunbridge Wells.

An East Surrey Traction Co. solid-tyred 'K' type open-top bus just managing to creep into this picture of the High Street in the late 1920s, quite probably to the annoyance of the photographer.

A funeral for a busman, Albert Ernest Powell, 12 October 1936. At the rear of the cortège as it passed through High Street was the preserved London General 'B' type No. B340, 'Ole Bill', driven by F. Cross. (H. Connold)

Hill Place viaduct, to the south of East Grinstead station, shortly before its completion in 1882. This drawing is in *The Life of Joseph Firbank* by F. McDermott, published in 1887.

The railway station building of 1882. Designed by T.H. Myres of Preston, it was destroyed by British Rail in 1971. The present prefabricated structure stands on its site.

A train bound for Three Bridges. This station, on the Three Bridges to Tunbridge Wells line, was in use from 1866 to 1883. The station building fronted on to London Road.

Kenneth Nutt, aged about 13, contemplating the Three Bridges to East Grinstead railway near Imberhorne, *c*. 1920. (Mrs N.F. Nutt)

Bert Buddle (left) and Harry Pavett (middle), two of H.H. Nutt's hire-car drivers, and a ticket collector, standing at the station entrance, 29 June 1923. The photographer originally captioned this picture 'Three Asses'! (K. Nutt)

A tank locomotive standing at the North signal cabin at the London end of the low-level station, after having worked the 3.36 p.m. train from Oxted, 1921. Porter-signalman George 'Juggy' Wren is watching from the balcony. (K. Nutt)

Signalman Tom Lammiman in the South signal cabin observing the arrival of the 1.25 p.m. Brighton to East Grinstead via Ardingly train, 5 October 1921. The signal cabin survived until July 1987. (K. Nutt)

Acknowledgements

Above all it is the talents of the early photographers whose work has been included in these pages, and credited when known, that must be acknowledged, for without that legacy a book of this nature would not be possible.

All photographs credited to Harold Connold are reproduced by courtesy of Malcolm Powell, his successor at No. 15 High Street, East Grinstead.

Much of the information in the captions is taken from *The History of East Grinstead* (W.H. Hills, 1906), from old street directories and local newspapers, and from the writings of the town's present historian, M.J. Leppard MA, to whom I am indebted for contributing the introduction and for checking my script.

My thanks go also to the trustees of East Grinstead Town Museum for making the photographs from its collection available for publication, and the museum's Hon. Curator, Dorothy Hatswell B.Ed., and Keith Brown for much advice and assistance in the preparation of *East Grinstead in Old Photographs*.

BRITAIN IN OLD PHOTOGRAPHS

To order any of these titles please telephone Littlehampton Book Services on 01903 721596

ALDERNEY

Alderney: A Second Selection, *B Bonnard*

BEDFORDSHIRE

Bedfordshire at Work, *N Lutt*

BERKSHIRE

Maidenhead, *M Hayles & D Hedges*
Around Maidenhead, *M Hayles & B Hedges*
Reading, *P Southerton*
Reading: A Second Selection, *P Southerton*
Sandhurst and Crowthorne, *K Dancy*
Around Slough, *J Hunter & K Hunter*
Around Thatcham, *P Allen*
Around Windsor, *B Hedges*

BUCKINGHAMSHIRE

Buckingham and District, *R Cook*
High Wycombe, *R Goodearl*
Around Stony Stratford, *A Lambert*

CHESHIRE

Cheshire Railways, *M Hitches*
Chester, *S Nichols*

CLWYD

Clwyd Railways, *M Hitches*

CLYDESDALE

Clydesdale, *Lesmahagow Parish Historical Association*

CORNWALL

Cornish Coast, *T Bowden*
Falmouth, *P Gilson*
Lower Fal, *P Gilson*
Around Padstow, *M McCarthy*
Around Penzance, *J Holmes*
Penzance and Newlyn, *J Holmes*
Around Truro, *A Lyne*
Upper Fal, *P Gilson*

CUMBERLAND

Cockermouth and District, *J Bernard Bradbury*
Keswick and the Central Lakes, *J Marsh*
Around Penrith, *F Boyd*
Around Whitehaven, *H Fancy*

DERBYSHIRE

Derby, *D Buxton*
Around Matlock, *D Barton*

DEVON

Colyton and Seaton, *T Gosling*
Dawlish and Teignmouth, *G Gosling*
Devon Aerodromes, *K Saunders*
Exeter, *P Thomas*
Exmouth and Budleigh Salterton, *T Gosling*
From Haldon to Mid-Dartmoor, *T Hall*
Honiton and the Otter Valley, *J Yallop*
Around Kingsbridge, *K Tanner*
Around Seaton and Sidmouth, *T Gosling*
Seaton, Axminster and Lyme Regis, *T Gosling*

DORSET

Around Blandford Forum, *B Cox*
Bournemouth, *M Colman*
Bridport and the Bride Valley, *J Burrell & S Humphries*
Dorchester, *T Gosling*
Around Gillingham, *P Crocker*

DURHAM

Darlington, *G Flynn*
Darlington: A Second Selection, *G Flynn*
Durham People, *M Richardson*
Houghton-le-Spring and Hetton-le-Hole, *K Richardson*
Houghton-le-Spring and Hetton-le-Hole:
   A Second Selection, *K Richardson*
Sunderland, *S Miller & B Bell*
Teesdale, *D Coggins*
Teesdale: A Second Selection, *P Raine*
Weardale, *J Crosby*
Weardale: A Second Selection, *J Crosby*

DYFED

Aberystwyth and North Ceredigion,
   Dyfed Cultural Services Dept
Haverfordwest, *Dyfed Cultural Services Dept*
Upper Tywi Valley, *Dyfed Cultural Services Dept*

ESSEX

Around Grays, *B Evans*

GLOUCESTERSHIRE

Along the Avon from Stratford to Tewkesbury, *J Jeremiah*
Cheltenham: A Second Selection, *R Whiting*
Cheltenham at War, *P Gill*
Cirencester, *J Welsford*
Around Cirencester, *E Cuss & P Griffiths*
Forest, The, *D Mullin*
Gloucester, *J Voyce*
Around Gloucester, *A Sutton*
Gloucester: From the Walwin Collection, *J Voyce*
North Cotswolds, *D Viner*
Severn Vale, *A Sutton*
Stonehouse to Painswick, *A Sutton*
Stroud and the Five Valleys, *S Gardiner & L Padin*
Stroud and the Five Valleys: A Second Selection,
   S Gardiner & L Padin
Stroud's Golden Valley, *S Gardiner & L Padin*
Stroudwater and Thames & Severn Canals,
   E Cuss & S Gardiner
Stroudwater and Thames & Severn Canals: A Second
   Selection, *E Cuss & S Gardiner*
Tewkesbury and the Vale of Gloucester, *C Hilton*
Thornbury to Berkeley, *J Hudson*
Uley, Dursley and Cam, *A Sutton*
Wotton-under-Edge to Chipping Sodbury, *A Sutton*

GWYNEDD

Anglesey, *M Hitches*
Gwynedd Railways, *M Hitches*
Around Llandudno, *M Hitches*
Vale of Conwy, *M Hitches*

HAMPSHIRE

Gosport, *J Sadden*
Portsmouth, *P Rogers & D Francis*

HEREFORDSHIRE

Herefordshire, *A Sandford*

HERTFORDSHIRE

Barnet, *I Norrie*
Hitchin, *A Fleck*
St Albans, *S Mullins*
Stevenage, *M Appleton*

ISLE OF MAN

The Tourist Trophy, *B Snelling*

ISLE OF WIGHT

Newport, *D Parr*
Around Ryde, *D Parr*

JERSEY

Jersey: A Third Selection, *R Lemprière*

KENT

Bexley, *M Scott*
Broadstairs and St Peter's, *J Whyman*
Bromley, Keston and Hayes, *M Scott*
Canterbury: A Second Selection, *D Butler*
Chatham and Gillingham, *P MacDougall*
Chatham Dockyard, *P MacDougall*
Deal, *J Broady*
Early Broadstairs and St Peter's, *B Wootton*
East Kent at War, *D Collyer*
Eltham, *J Kennett*
Folkestone: A Second Selection, *A Taylor & E Rooney*
Goudhurst to Tenterden, *A Guilmant*
Gravesend, *R Hiscock*
Around Gravesham, *R Hiscock & D Grierson*
Herne Bay, *J Hawkins*
Lympne Airport, *D Collyer*
Maidstone, *I Hales*
Margate, *R Clements*
RAF Hawkinge, *R Humphreys*
RAF Manston, *RAF Manston History Club*
RAF Manston: A Second Selection,
   RAF Manston History Club
Ramsgate and Thanet Life, *D Perkins*
Romney Marsh, *E Carpenter*
Sandwich, *C Wanostrocht*
Around Tonbridge, *C Bell*
Tunbridge Wells, *M Rowlands & I Beavis*
Tunbridge Wells: A Second Selection,
   M Rowlands & I Beavis
Around Whitstable, *C Court*
Wingham, Adisham and Littlebourne, *M Crane*

LANCASHIRE

Around Barrow-in-Furness, *J Garbutt & J Marsh*
Blackpool, *C Rothwell*
Bury, *J Hudson*
Chorley and District, *J Smith*
Fleetwood, *C Rothwell*
Heywood, *J Hudson*
Around Kirkham, *C Rothwell*
Lancashire North of the Sands, *J Garbutt & J Marsh*
Around Lancaster, *S Ashworth*
Lytham St Anne's, *C Rothwell*
North Fylde, *C Rothwell*
Radcliffe, *J Hudson*
Rossendale, *B Moore & N Dunnachie*

LEICESTERSHIRE

Around Ashby-de-la-Zouch, *K Hillier*
Charnwood Forest, *I Keil, W Humphrey & D Wix*
Leicester, *D Burton*
Leicester: A Second Selection, *D Burton*
Melton Mowbray, *T Hickman*
Around Melton Mowbray, *T Hickman*
River Soar, *D Wix, P Shacklock & I Keil*
Rutland, *T Clough*
Vale of Belvoir, *T Hickman*
Around the Welland Valley, *S Mastoris*

LINCOLNSHIRE

Grimsby, *J Tierney*
Around Grimsby, *J Tierney*
Grimsby Docks, *J Tierney*
Lincoln, *D Cuppleditch*